UNTYING THE KNOT

UNTYING THE KNOT

Karen Paul Holmes

Aldrich Press

For Sayanne,

Such a total
pleasure to have
you in class —

keep going with
your beautiful
writing &
reading!

XOXO
Karen

ISBN 13: 978-0615998985

Cover art: Katja Holmes

Kelsay Books
Aldrich Press
24600 Mountain Avenue, 35
Hemet, California 92544

This book is dedicated to my mother, Elva Paul, who passed away during the writing of these poems.

Contents

After: Photos of Me and Other Possibilities

Before: Waking Without Alarm

Drawn into Circles

Last evening, I placed fresh towels on both dog beds
heard scratching and rearranging in the night.
This morning, each dog lay curled
into a circle of towel
like a bird's nest.

How life loves
a circle:
the sun
cups of tea
pizza, roses, embraces
wedding rings, cathedral domes, bells
with notes radiating like ripples from skipped stones
the egg, the womb, the opening, downy heads
suckling mouths, breasts, eyes filled
with delight for bubbles
and bouncing balls.

Why do we box ourselves into corners
put our babies into rectangular cribs
build square houses and boxy buildings
drive cars to perpendicular crossroads
stare at newspapers, monitors, dollars
go to our rest in hard-edged coffins
slowly lowered into matching graves?

It's a comfort
to imagine our rounded bones
becoming round bits of the globe
our spirits rising to orbit among spiral galaxies
joining those who completed the circle before us.

Waking Without Alarm

a day without obligations
slivers of silver spilling from the shades
a small ceremony of jasmine tea in the Japanese pot
ten minutes of Qi Gong, twenty rubbing Watson's belly
in the evening, a pang of regret for a lazy day
then remembering
I deserve a chance to do something or nothing
innate joy rising
and Watson, smiling, asleep in his basket.

Bargaining with Karma

Dear Karma, you can have my Girl Scout badges
if I can take back shunning Ann Sanders next door

Giggles at *Catcher in the Rye*
for savoring *Valley of the Dolls*

I'll give back almost anything except time with my dogs
for things I did in college (you know what I'm saying)

I could also give up working at Petite Shoppe
for asking a woman if she was pregnant when she wasn't

The King & I revival on Broadway?—
not worth throwing up in the theatre lobby

Yes, I enjoyed Amanda's dinner party once I got there
but not driving off with my peach pie on the car's roof

Please take back that carat ring my husband gave me
and return his mother's small gold necklace I lost

And here is whatever pleasure I had shopping
the day I picked up my daughter late on her birthday

Thanks for stuff that seemed dreadful but really wasn't:
    seeing my parents drive away from Camp Fair Winds
    my first wedding cancelled after I got the dress
    two lay-offs from big, "important" jobs
    even my fall from a deck eight feet up

In fact, why mess with the dominoes—
their pockmarked, yet magnificent faces?

Life, Act 3

—to my husband, Nov. 2009

Time knows its lines
has spoken them
across our foreheads.
In this stage of living
we censor the critic,
applaud the comedy,
watch the script unfold.
Gravity plays upon
these bodies, while
souls move inward,
heavenward.
The star in me
celebrates the star in you.

During: Beyond My Ken

Help Interpret the Symbolism in Mrs. Why's True Story

—March 2010

She stares at a pile of her husband's dirty laundry
while he spends a trial weekend with "Mrs. X."
The wife has suddenly become "Mrs. Why."
There can be a fine line between doing the noble thing

and being a push-over. Does she take this heap
of obvious symbolism, wash it, dry it, leave it
in a neat little pile for his return?
He believes Mrs. Why is a good woman.
That's why he's loved her for 31 years.

Now, she has bowed aside for this tryst, hoping
fervor will burn out. He believes it might,
but he's not sure. X, by the way,
was Mrs. Why's trusted friend until last week.

Mrs. Why feels a hurricane pounding her.
Knowing she should care for herself,
she blends a protein shake,
anger whirs on high as she tries to forgive.

Last night she dreamed of him with X:
He's paying for a hotel, $500 a day.
Suddenly, Mrs. Why is on the toilet, but X demands,
Get up! It's my turn. The bathroom fills with people;
Mrs. Why asks, *Am I on Candid Camera?*
Yes! And you've won fabulous prizes!

Months later, Mr. and Mrs. Why continue to receive
bags of onions they won. The promised cash
never comes. Of course, there's allegory here,
but what do the onions mean?
An old and useful ingredient?
A taste that stays on the tongue?

Suddenly, Old-Fashioned Words Apply to Me

Betrayed
Scorned
Divorcée

The self-help book even calls me
cuckold

My man found a *convenient*
gave her the *green gown*
gave me no suffrage in the matter

He claims I've been coddled
corseted, not *harlot* enough…
Now my mirror reduces me
to a *blowsabella*

I'd rather be damsel
or lady in waiting

for a swashbuckler
to swing
                from a chandelier
his horse ready
below
the third floor window
as we leap

and land
smack
in the saddle
for a just-in-time escape
dashing away, me hanging on
                to my dear
                        dear life…

Beyond My Ken

ken
noun: knowledge, cognizance; mental perception.
verb: to know, have knowledge of or about, or be acquainted with
proper noun: short form of Kenneth

without, i fail the test
words fail me
i lose the combination
scribble circles
can't draw conclusions
heart becomes prune
then pit

i drift
no anchor
rudder
compass
chart

the bottom tempts me

my feet flop
train's derailed
balloon leaks
plane won't lift
i wander useless roads
on a bike with one tire
every light, red

Ken navigates another now
they're 100 miles down the path.

To She Who Will Not be Named

Part of me wants to wish you the worst:
silicone sacs ruptured
(breasts drooping to your hip bones),
butt spread across Georgia,
the gym you own boarded up—
malpractice pending.
But instead, I wish you what I endured:
him supine on your couch,
book in his face ten hours a day.
Why would it be different at your house?
Smell his cigar-breath kisses.
Hear him argue with waitresses
about expired coupons.
Sense his disapproval
of your extra five pounds.
At night, fall into cold ceramic
when he leaves the seat up.

I watch you overlook his flaws,
as you believe he overlooks yours.
I see tears springing to your eyes,
when he springs the news of his new love,
a friend of yours.
He will say he's justified because you
haven't made him happy in years.
I feel the pulsing current of your grief.
I perceive your puzzlement
at the arguments you and he never had.
I listen in as you try to explain the concept
of forgiveness to your daughter
(but no, you have no child as he and I do).

I watch you pathetically hiding the shirt
you thought he looked sexy in—
moving it way to the back of the closet—
so he can't pack it among everything else
he's taking away.

I'm Really Not Crazy, but She Is

This is going to sound strange
but I think the jewelry my friend made me was cursed.
Necklaces of sodalite, lapis, rose quartz beads
Swarovski crystal earrings, blood red for Valentine's
and a little note, *with loving kindness from C—.*
All, she claimed, vibrated energies to benefit me.
Never quite my style, but it's the thought that counts:
She wanted my husband.
Within two years of the "gifts":
One of our dogs almost died
his body attacking its own red cells.
The other dislocated her hip—
surgery involving rods
and reshaping bone.
My husband had his thyroid removed
and started sleeping with his natural healer (C—).
His niece's husband committed suicide.
His sister died of lymphoma, but before that,
her dear friend had a stroke
in the middle of the night while visiting us.
My mother's lymphoma returned
and killed her.
My brother had bladder cancer surgery
then a staph infection.
But silly me, I still have the jewelry.
Shoved it in a plastic bag when my husband sprung
the news. Didn't have the heart to give it away
and cause someone else such trouble.
Today (!) I'm taking the baubles to a thrift shop
having first blessed them any way I could.
May someone wear them in peace.
May my family's peace begin again.
May the curse not travel through this poem to you.

Rumination

I wish I could cut off my head
or at least open it a crack
to let all these thoughts fly
into another galaxy
where they could be put to use
in some soap opera
comedy of errors
theatre of the absurd
epic tragedy
morality play
or even a silly song
about a cow chewing his cud
He said...
I said...
If only he...
If only I...
Why?
Why?
Why?

Mantra Trouble at the Meditation Retreat

—On a mountaintop near Asheville, NC

The yogi Dada teaches us to silently focus
breathe in: Baba Nam
breathe out: Kevalam

Baba Nam Kevalam
Baba Lam Kevala
Baba Yam Kavala
No, that's not right!
Baba   NAM   Ke va LAM

Sanskrit vibrations supposedly
mesh body and universe,
help us connect with oneness,
withdraw mind from external world.

Baba NAM KevaLAM!
Baba   Nam   Ke va lam
Baba Lam Kevela

It's doing the opposite.
Mantra monotony makes thoughts flow,
repetition stirs nerves,
twists my mental tongue.
I'm multi-tasking instead of meditating.
Baba Lam, I mean Nam… when will it end?

Baba Nam means *Infinite Light Feeling*
Kevalam means *Only*.
I switch to English, but it has no rhythm—
breaths should be equal.
I give up and just feel.
Light and peace fill me.

In comes a singer with guitar.
We all sing O Baba Nam-ah Kevalam-ah
More syllables to confuse,
and now melody too, plus a dance:
toe tap right, toe tap left
arms raised, eyes closed.
O Baba Nam-ah Kevalam-ah
O Baba Lam-ah Kevalam-ah

My arms hurt.
I open eyes to spy—everyone seems into it.
I've moved far to one side,
near collision with my neighbor,
another worry.

O Baba Nam-ah Kevalam-ah
O Baba Lam-ah Kevalam-ah
ad infinitum

What if Baba Lam means darkness?
And did I mention I'm fasting?
I think of the **broth** for dinner,
now 40 minutes late.
(Note to retreat planners:
Don't let meditation come between fasters and broth).

Later, I find others have trouble
with Baba Nam Kevalam too,
even my most spiritual friend.
(She said it was a little too Hare Krishna for her).
I feel exonerated, though now I must work on my need
to be perfect, my tendency to judge.

Next day,
I skip the meditation,
take a walk instead.
Stones on the path and a cardinal's red flash
speak to me like Baba Lam Kevala never did.
I mean Baba NAM Ke va LAM.

Burned

I pen those hate letters
long and hard.
To him, who betrayed me,
to her, my friend who kissed
me like a female Judas.
The therapist said it would move me
through grief, and so I spit
onto the yellow legal pad—
streams of malice blasts
gall, vitriol
fits of *damns, bitches, bastards.*

Now I burn the letters—
they smolder but don't want to catch.
It takes fifteen big kitchen matches
to destroy ten pages on the stones in my drive.
Then strikes of match after match
to cremate *her* letter.
A spark ignites the dry leaves a foot away—
I stomp and stomp them out.
Another match finishes her final
browned corner: I have to smile
as the last tenacious ash floats,
disappears.

Am I Doing this Grieving Thing Correctly?

I throw eggs against a tree
as my Buddhist counselor suggests.

I write, then burn, letters
as my therapist instructs.

I meditate,
sit with the sadness, don't resist.

I'm a straight-A student
trying to master this hellish test.

And still,
even in restaurants, the grocery,

I'm like my sister who cried all over her
Mexican village the year Manolo left:

The children began to call her *La Llorona*,
The Weeping Woman.

The Tongue of Love

Do you speak it long and lusciously
rolling Rs and stretching syllables?
Do you make it rise like a question?
Or say it with weight.
Precisely pronounced?
Tumbled rapidly?
With accent?
Clipped?
A drone?
A shout?
A whisper?
A sign?
A song?

I spoke it prayerfully in my head,
thought he went to that silent place with me.

Extraneous Catherine

Where is the manual?
I want to put parts
A
and
B
back together.
Part C doesn't belong:
I'd like to wrench
her with a hex.

It took three score to construct
this structure;
one night to deconstruct.
I have no instructions
for troubleshooting,
no crude drawing showing
how to connect broken

connections.
Just blinking   red   lights
blinking   blinking.

My lifetime guarantee
has not been honored.
I don't want a refund—
just need to be A
reinforced by B again,
even if slightly damaged.
A replacement part will not do.

Compassion

—to my separated husband

Is it still damp
or just cold,
this pillow you filled
with tears?
Let me lay my face there
that I may absorb your sorrow.
Let me press my self into the still-warm place
where your body felt alone.
I will pull the blanket of your anguish over me
and remember this lesson
if there's a next time.

Telling My Mother

—after Sharon Olds

She's 85. Upsets make her heart palpitate
so we couch what we say. Or maybe we always have.
Now that Ken's been gone six weeks
my siblings and I confer on how to tell her
that he left me.
She loves him.

I wait until my sister travels to Florida
as back-up support for Mother, then call. Hear myself
somehow keep my voice from quaking.
He wants to separate for a while… depressed
since thyroid surgery. I think
he'll be back.

She's sad for me but surprisingly supportive.
Motherly. Modern. *Sometimes couples do well*
with a break: Their marriage becomes stronger.
I didn't know any of her friends did that
but I believe her.

She visits me in Appalachia a few months later.
As we walk by the lake, he calls my cell. Some business
item to discuss. As usual, we try to keep a light note.
He chirps, *Say hi to Baba.*
(The name our daughter calls her.)
I cannot say to him
You've broken Baba's heart too.

I put the phone in my back pocket
take her thin hand, let her rest on a fieldstone bench.
To her questioning face, I tell a small lie
His calls don't bother me anymore.
I do not give her his regards.

Next day, she and I are driving
the two hours back to my mountain cabin after I'd read
at an Asheville bookstore. Before we get
to the hairpin curves, it suddenly feels right to say
He had an affair.
He lives with her now.

She's not surprised. Maybe by 85 she's heard it all.
My contact lenses fogging, the road is a blur, but no
slowing down *She was my good friend.*
Mother, angry now, controlled
He never loved you enough.
He expected you to be perfect.

Though I know the route, I get lost—
we pass thick dark pines, cliffs, the fast Nantahala,
feel lucky for this scenic detour.
At home, I sense a burden was tumbled
clean in the rapids, washed
down that river.

One Step Forward: Reality Show:
Save This Marriage

Thirty-Second Anniversary

—February 2011

Sometimes a husband will invite you,
haltingly, to have dinner on February 24th.
Your heart does a little salsa and nods *yes.*
Brain strategizes, *Play hard to get.*
But how do you play teenage games now?
How do you hide your feelings when your therapist
encourages you to show vulnerability?
After a marriage of independence, how do you mold
yourself into what he wants you to be?
After a year of trying to believe you're better off
alone, how do you ask him to change the things
you know need changing?
Sometimes a husband says, *We don't need therapy.*
Sometimes you reluctantly agree
though it feels like you'll be trying
to drag a whale across sand.

Dilemma

To have sex or not to have sex.
That is the question...

Rug

A striking silk Persian
600 knots in each inch.
Carmine and ivory arabesques,
indigo tendrils.
Too bad about the bulge—
thirty years of marital debris.
We've swept
the surface
but never aired it out.
To me, it's a molehill;
we could uncover,
inspect, solve.
To you, it's a risky height,
not worth the stifling climb.

Reality Show: Save This Marriage

Platform covered with eggshells
shaking like a Richter 8 earthquake.
Your challenge: Walk across
without crushing any.
Alligator pit comes next,
fifty-foot poles sway on either side
tightrope strung across, covered
with bear grease.
No safety harness, and of course
no net.
Still in the game?
Now for the intellectual challenge.
You have five minutes to assemble
a 1,000-piece puzzle, but
your husband's got half the pieces
locked in a safe
at the bottom of the Tasmanian Sea.
Fail, and he votes you off the show.

Shoulda Woulda Coulda

Didn't.

Now get on with it.

Two Steps Back: If Left to Your Own Devices

How to Undo a Kiss

—June 2011

withdraw tongue
slowly slide lips together, then
    release his
remove fingers from his hair
un-caress neck
pull your body away
 from
  all
    the places
     it
       touches his.

Untying the Knot

Bitter end: The loose end of a rope.

Why do knots form by themselves?
In my blow dryer cord,
cell phone charger,
dog leashes.
What Boy Scout crept into the dark
to practice right over left
around and through?
And what of the sheepshank of worry
in my stomach,
muscles tied tense with monkey's fists,
hair tangled in little nooses?

The twists and hitches in our relationship—
who caused those?
Should I have jumped
through one more hoop
to tighten our ties,
looped my love around you
one more time?
Like a rope,
our marriage failed at the stress of the knot
and frayed at the bitter end.

The Faceting of Forever

Start
with carbon.
Bury it ninety miles beneath
the earth's crust, in the mantle
under continental plates.

Apply
five gigapascals of pressure.
Bake at two thousand degrees
for a million years or more.

Wait
for volcanic action to push
the cargo upward.
Allow to cool, solidify.

Mine.
Cut fifty-eight facets.
Count the carats.
Classify the clarity.

Marvel
that black matter
in a black hole
can become colorless brilliance.
Admire the fire when the stone
disperses light into a spectrum.

Fashion
onto a circle of platinum.
Feel the strength
to ward off suitors.
Place on the left ring finger
over the vein that runs to the heart.

A diamond can cut anything,
even cleave rock-hard faith
when the circle moves
from left hand   to   right
severing   *forever.*

And So it Comes to This

We face each other at the mahogany table,
papers spread. I'd already asked to put this off
when Mother was ill, again because she died.
Ken had agreed: In most things, he was a nice guy.

But this doesn't feel nice. I feels like a fight,
a movie scene: The woman who's playing me has lines
across her gray forehead, fingers pick at cuticles.
And how can that blank face be my Ken?

Maybe I should've hired the bulldog: Eva
in her glass and steel tower with a view of everything.
She had riled me up (I should get far more than 50%
from that cheating man). But mascara bled,
dripped on the drive home:

I'd spilled trade secrets to a bulldog, plotted
behind Ken's back, the man who shared most
of my years, assets hard won for our future, a child.
I threatened him with Eva but knew he was right
to sneer, *The only ones who'll win are the lawyers.*

So we'd agreed to find fair attorneys: Kind Eileen
sits next to me. I thought I was ready, safe—yet feel
like a knife thrower's target, spinning on a wheel,
arms and legs splayed as in da Vinci's drawing.
At each meeting, another hit to the gut.

The harder I try to tit-for-tat, the tougher Ken is.
I remember the book on taking the high road
in divorce, know if I go that route, he will too.
I do. Relief, small smiles, a pretty fair deal.
I look forward to the end…

But the drafted papers jab, *as if the marriage
never occurred.* Those words recorded for perpetuity?
I have them deleted. When Ken proposed,
he'd said, *Grow old with me.*
We don't look at each other as we sign.

I wait for court approval: Thirty days slip
to forty-five. On an ordinary day,
the certified decree arrives. I touch its raised seal.
That's all I feel.

Mr. Divorce Jimmied the Back Door

Of course, he came to rob
to take my peace of mind.
But why did he stay?
My frantic calls to 911 failed.

I feel his eye
at the keyhole as I bathe.
Did the curtains just move?
Why is the fridge door open,
milk nearly gone?

At night
he becomes a cloaked figure,
breath blowing cold. Like a dementor
Mr. D attempts to suck hope
right out of me.

In daylight, he's a nuisance
gloating over my shoulder
as I get up with the dogs at dawn
grill my own steak
plunge the toilet.
Rap rattles my cup and saucer
cigar ash smears mahogany, sooty
footprints mount the carpeted stairs.
And still, his shadow startles me
in every room.

My Perfect House on the Market

The doggie door is too small for one couple's mastiff, a retired
man's two old golden retrievers have bad knees and can't do stairs,
a woman with bad knees can't afford an elevator but loves the
ambiance, a gay designer feels the foyer staircase looks out of
proportion. Though most think the kitchen large, an entertaining
wife says it's smallish. One person would paint the oak raised-
panel family room white but doesn't make an offer. The offer of a
New Orleans litigator is abhorrently low. He won't budge. My
husband decided the rooms of our marriage, which suited us for
decades, no longer fit.

My Stew

tastes like an old shoe
with spicy nuances
a family recipe
of oral tradition

stir up bitter leftovers
aged beefs
rosemary and its memories
onions full of tears

simmer for days
with a splash of whine
bring to a rolling boil
savor its sauciness

freeze it, reheat it, spit
it from your lips
or dump it, grind it, scrub
its dregs from the pot

better yet, skip to dessert
swirl it and smooth it, make
it your signature dish
call it My Chocolate Bliss.

How to Make Lemonade

Take your sour experience,
water it down with detached observation,
squeeze out bitterness through acceptance.
Add the sweetness of knowing it's only life unfolding.
Balance your glass on the window sill between past
and future, fill with sparrow song, gardenias,
stones from an icy stream.
Drink in all the wisdom you can.

Zumba with Lady Gaga

—divorce therapy

A week ago, I didn't know Lady Gaga
from Lady Godiva.
Now I'm stumbling through
a fusion of Latin, hip-hop, belly and pop
while Gaga rocks her lyrics right at me:
She still loves her Judas too.
After three Zumba classes I'm keeping up—
salsa, samba, and the Kumbia Kings:
Fuego! The roof's burnin' but we don't care.
Bollywood, calypso, soca, reggaeton
(faster now; heart rate up!)
Step on the *gasolina:* My baby likes *gasolina!*
(or something like that).
I'm told some of the words are dirty—luckily
(or un), I don't know Spanish, Arabic, Hindi
and can't catch half the English.
Panting, we take it down a notch to the lyric
I'm lookin' for a Jack who's not a ripper.
Then: right foot cha cha cha
left foot cha cha cha
turn turn turn turn
           step right
step left
swim, monkey, frugue, pony.
Our 20-ish teacher calls this one "the '80s"
but I recall go-go boots in sixth grade, 1966.
Now it's, "Bring out your inner Beyoncé!"
for *Single Ladies*, the only song I knew before.
More mambo, tango and a peppy meringue rap:
the guy has passion in his pants
and likes to flaunt it.

Miraculously, I can now shimmy.
Mirrors line one wall.
That's me smilin', sweatin', hot
pink tank, black tights—
like the last song says,
I'm groovin' my rock moves
and I don't need
him
tonight.

If Left to Your Own Devices

What would you do?
I'd stay up late
watching *Slings & Arrows*
or *Sex in the City*
episode after episode
or compose poems or
list things to do tomorrow
… never do them
because I'd sleep late,
take a nap,
stay on the computer too long.
I'd order in light gourmet
and try to avoid junk food
(I don't consider chocolate
junk, but please keep
the Cheetos away).
My Pilates coach would
come to the house
and make my stomach flat.
I'd see my roses but not the weeds,
watch currents skim the lake
but ignore the eroding shore;
I might even wade neck deep…
I'd convince myself
that it's nice by.myself,
and since the impossibly bad
had the audacity to happen,
then it's possible
the impossibly good
will show up soon.

After: Photos of Me and Other Possibilities

Visitor

A bare branch lounges
in my Adirondack chair
under the Japanese maple—
gray, elegant:
Comforting to me,
now without a husband,
a good omen
in my walled garden
cocooned by snow.

Surrendering

God must have a gigantic box
half the size of the universe
or heaven.
Where else would He store all
I've given Him lately?
The pain-fear-anger of divorce
the grief of mother's death
brother's cancer
the stiff-lipped good bye
of my daughter's move.
He locks that box up tight
but sometimes, through cracks
I drag out the garments
wear their weight
for moments or days.
Why indulge
in such addiction to suffering?
Better to look at each,
feel the tight threads, rough warp,
then surrender them for good.

Healing in Cedar Hedge Garden

—Interlochen, Michigan, 2011

My sister sketched the garden's wood
and rusty metal gate
last week on the day Mother died.
She and I return now, settle onto a dappled bench
near a pond with three fountains,
one a fat bronze Buddha.
Eileen draws, I write.
Water spills in counterpoint
to wind chimes throughout the acreage:

Near us, a silver soprano
meets the susurrus of trees, viburnum, long grasses.
Mezzos reach our ears from all directions
in unplanned harmony.
Larger than me, the dark metal tubes
of the far-off basso vibrate,
more feeling than sound.

Hostas surround us.
Collected over twenty years: eight hundred varieties
eight hundred greens, leaves of all sizes.
A few sport slanting purple flowers this late August
near my sister's home and the Sleeping Bear dunes.

I wasn't ready to return south alone
wearing another loss like a chainmail shawl.
Eileen lightens me.
We usually chatter
but now sit, silent,
let the garden do its work.

Fall

Despite the wind
poplars hang on to their leaves.
They catch the light and flutter like gilded eyelids,
jiggle like coins on a belly dancer's hip scarf.
Whitecaps jostle my dock,
lake darker than the sky.
Those distant mountains, dusty-red with autumn,
recall Sedona's rocks,
but green grass and willows speak
of lush Appalachia.

Joy surges
mixed with the old longing: that need to share.
The cherry tree over there—blooming
and showing orange foliage at the same time—
must be as confused as I am
since the gusty lusty breath of Catherine
blew away the colors of my marriage,
forced the black and white of divorce.

Suddenly, a shower of acorns bounces
off my head, knocking me back
into the windy, sunny present.

Mating Instincts

I'm not ready to jump
on the find-a-man bandwagon.
Haven't had to since 25—
when (it's said) my instincts chose
a mate whose genes mixed
with mine for the best offspring.
Yep, got a check-plus, gold star there.

What might I want at 56?
Rather than a handsome face,
long legs, high IQ, maybe
it's wisdom, longevity,
no adult son
still at home addicted
to *Star Trek* reruns.
But some men my age look like
how I remember Grandpa
(usually dozing in his chair):
wisps of yellow-white hair, scalp
spotted, Basset jowls, ear lobes
to his collar bones.
I can still smell the Old Spice…

Yet coupling instincts run strong.
With a mind of their own,
my eyes scan the left hand
of every man,
even those least likely—
my mother's greasy-haired,
stressed-out gastroenterologist;

the 40-ish guy in red pants
pressing the elevator button;
the sewer repairman who,
at first heart-stopping glance,
looks like the one
whose midlife crisis caused mine.

Lunching with the Devil

I'll admit, I invited him
(met him online;
always had a thing for bad boys).
Reaching Dante's Dining Den,
I ask angels for an invisible shield.
To keep myself grounded,
I visualize my chakras spinning clockwise
from root to crown—
I am ready.
He walks in, not red, just a little sunburned,
dark hair plastered down like Alfalfa's,
suit slightly wrinkled, thin red tie,
pocket square with a chili pepper print.
Oddly attractive, the kind of crooked smile
and lanky body I like.
My shield holds—
he doesn't shake hands,
let alone kiss my cheek.
The menu busies us.
He eyes the waitress like she's a marshmallow
he wants to roast.
Orders peppercorn sirloin with sizzling rice.
I stick to salad.
He raves about his Aspen condo,
but complains of the cold.
Tells me to invest in AT&T.
Says he rather likes global warming.
In time, I ask, *Do you have any regrets about Eve?*
He says, *Sometimes I feel a twinge.*

Me: *What about segregation, oil spills, child abuse?*
And if God is in everything, is God in you?
He has to look away.
After a moment, he winks,
asks me to the Do Drive-In
to see *Simply Irresistible* on Friday.
Our waitress interrupts with the dessert tray.
Him: *Can I tempt you into sharing Molten Lava Cake?*
Me: *Just a refill of iced tea, please.*

At home, a swift click of the mouse
changes my identity.
I sigh to my dog, *I'm not* that *lonely.*

White after Memorial Day

It's only April 10th, yet I've shimmied
into optic white jeans, rejoicing
they fit from last summer; white
doesn't forgive. Boiling
for broth on the stove: the chaff
of last night's chicken
thyme rubbed into its olive-oiled skin
for my dinner party
where a true Belle told me, *In the South, you go*
by temperature not date.
In Michigan this wouldn't happen
and even here, I don't wear white shoes
until June first. I just won't.
A Charleston gentleman, 82, with young man's glasses
asked me to coffee. He heard of my divorce.
I refused, politely. His wife died three years ago.
Twin Cadillacs, circa 1980, sit in his carport
side by side, limo-long and white.

Photos of Me and Other Possibilities

Framed, me at 26, Golden Gate Park, 1980
    windy-haired, pretty
in white sequins with our pink moiré Katie
my headshot when I became a VP
the updated one he took for my speaking gigs
    (with digital camera, 40 tries to satisfy me)
the black-and-white with our Welsh Terrier pup
my short hair, my long hair, in sunglasses, in profile
always smiling. Genuinely? I think so.

They're all he left when he packed his desk, 2011.
I pull out of the drive, a possibility dawns:
His basement office could be my exercise room.
No cold car heading to Pilates. I could add a sauna
to his bathroom. And maybe I should park
on each side of the garage 50/50
so that the automatic doors will wear evenly
now that the whole place is mine.

Has He Landed Safely?

I worry that the outstretched legs on the hart are bent the wrong way
as he throws himself off.
   —from *Stag's Leap*, Sharon Olds

Not at all a graceful takeoff
his leap threw him into the wild blue
ambiguity of an affair.
I now know he had to do it:
had to explore, sail off the edge
of the world.

I now know he had one limb out
of our marriage for years.
Kept trying to balance
his accounts—in his mind
he and I did not equal happiness
even though I was the wife he wanted
to show. Smart,
pretty enough, a good mother.
He loved me as much as he could
but I did not fill his coffers.

For two years he resisted the lure
of her but it persisted,
a bee in his palm,
until he couldn't hold it any longer.
He was barely more than fawn
in the ways of betrayal, antlers
uncalcified. Yet he craved
the danger, needed it
like heroin to addle his pain.

He had to leap, to deny the gravity
of his action. To land, gashed
in another galaxy.
Does he speak the language?
Can he breathe?

71

Photos of My Ex on the Internet

Sometimes I can't resist spying on my ex's girlfriend
by visiting her blog. There she is doing yoga poses.
I see her xeriscaped garden, orchids in her studio
where we used to sit and gossip. When she posted
a photo of him, the caption, *My little family,*
coiled my gut. Could he just switch families after
thirty years with me, our daughter, our dogs?
But there is his hurry-take-the-photo smile,
more wrinkles than I remember,
in the shirt I bought. Her sad-faced, red-eyed
dog (that he'd always disliked) sits on his lap.
She stands over him, hands on both his shoulders.

A few months later, I discover her family reunion:
He's small in the back row of fourteen people
on a beach, but I recognize his posture before I blow up
the photo. Wind tossing hair, he looks happier, perhaps
heavier: jaw tucked back from the camera
makes a double chin. His hand's on the top
of her wicker chair—there's a gap between her head/
his chest. Her half-smile looks like resignation.
Or maybe it's peace, or maybe a nanosecond nothing
as the shutter clicked.

She wears yoga pants under her sundress, though others
have on shorts, t-shirts. Probably she performed poses
on the beach—typical of her: partly spiritual, partly
show-offy. I hope she's gained weight, especially
in her arms, but it may be the angle. She always
claimed to be estranged from her family. Have they
accepted her now that she has a nice, *normal* boyfriend,
finally divorced?

It seems like I hate her, doesn't it? Let's just say
I believe she's disappointed, which makes me smirk
a bit. I'd like to be a knot on her wood-paneled wall
to study how they get along. I peer into the photos,
looking, so I can say *I told you so.* But no,
I'd like him to be happy… with a half pinch of regret.
Here's one from Christmas: They're down-wrapped
on a cruise ship deck, Antarctica's white stretching
behind them. She loves penguins, and though he never
could take the cold, he stands there beside her,
his smile frozen.

Komodo

You don't have to hate the Komodo dragon,
but you don't have to get into its cage either.
—David R. Hawkins, MD

O friend who is now Komodo to me
I don't blame you for loving the man
I loved—he's Rhett Butler handsome
with that sly smile when he laughs
at his own jokes. He can be kind, sexy.
He'll be easy to live with if your passion
matches his, but beware the electric
current of his criticism. It can burn.

O friend, we once had girl-crushes
on each other—debated the merits
of high heels, did Qi Gong, shared
gluten-free recipes, grumbled a bit
about our men. Last time I saw you,
I didn't know you'd slept with mine.

Was it hard to act normal? You said
the pain between my shoulder blades
might be stress over work. My psyche
must have known: Next day, I found out
you'd knifed me. What in you allowed
your betrayal? You live with it now
and with a man heavy under his guilt.

Remember the teachings we studied,
you and he and I? We all do the best
we're capable of at the time. I believe
you only did what you could… just
as I cannot tell you in person I forgive
you, though I do, as much as I'm able
in this moment…

While Master Chen guides me
to *Push Up the Heavens*...
lift my palms from heart to sky,
exhale, lower, repeat.

Three White Gowns

on headless mannequins in the window for two years.
One has gray water stains seeping up its hem.
Inside, chandeliers light a handful of strapless satin

ghosts dangling in a niche on the left wall.
I walk by this swank storefront on Peachtree daily,
a sign swings from a grosgrain bow, says, *Closed*

in script curling like tendrils around a bride's face.
It feels as if the owner simply moved on. Divorced,
a friend wrote a poem about her gown being tossed

in a pile when she took it to Goodwill. My sister
didn't mind seeing her own dress—wrinkled, ripped
after daughters, then grands had played bride,

though I felt a pang—I helped her choose it
and the veiled, vintage hat to match. She said she
never thinks about her ex now. Will that be me?

My gown moved with my then-husband and me
from home to home. Last year, I brought it here—
to my own place. Yet, I can't ask my daughter

whether she'll want to wear it: sweetheart neckline,
Chantilly sleeves to the wrist. A tuck at the waist
would cinch it to her thinness, and she likes tradition.

Or is it something now of bad luck that can't be
annulled by a sixpence rubbing in her shoe? Not sure
how I'd feel watching her walk the aisle in it, perhaps

a few years from now. Her father, if he's there, might
look at her; think of me. No, not my desire. Let it wait
in another closet, yellowing for someone else.

From a Faraway Place, I Write to My Daughter

Today the sky is pearl gray, backlit
so that its brightness still begs sunglasses.
Trees and grasses seem to fluoresce.
Everything looks christened by rain,
no sun to undermine color.

Around the pool,
begonias' pink blooms, bronze leaves thrive
along with healthy purple flowers—
I don't know their names.
Red brick townhouses gleam against black asphalt.
I look upon oddly slanted roofs above white sidewalks
with boxwood borders.

My Welsh Terriers see this out the window
and do not bark at strangers. No one is strange here.
No insects bite or sting. Chiming music floats
from somewhere quite near. Bells, flutes,
a toy piano perhaps—
I spent the morning dancing around my room,
wearing a blue bra and lace panties
(they don't match, but they're pretty).
My hair, now the shining blonde of childhood,
has grown past my waist.

I see you are well, my darling. Please write
to your father at his last known address:
He's still there. Tell him
you forgive him for leaving me.
Tell him I've learned to waltz.

Birthday Gift to Self

—April 1, 2012

I'm still in my robe at 2 p.m.
though dishes removed from the sold sideboard
need to be bubble wrapped and snuggled
into U-Haul boxes my new man brought me.
Five miles of *to do's* before I move
to my downsized home. At least
dinner is set—
he shops now, will cook tonight.
Midweek he told me
to wear a nice dress on Saturday.
He'd put on his gray-blue suit.
The surprise? Tango
salsa, waltz until midnight
we lost our shoes to appease our burning feet,
began in unison to hanker
for BLTs. He manned my stove. I toasted
rye bread, spread mayo, sliced a purple tomato.

Now Sunday, full of spring
birthday of nobody's fool—
Dogs wag at me for their 'round-the-block walk
but I allow my fingers to foxtrot
across the laptop keys,
printer hot with poetry.

Does Unconditional Love Include Hawaiian Shirts?

The olive one has orange hibiscus with faces
like the monsters I imagined in my mom's
bedroom wallpaper.

The second: green and brown palm trees against
fuchsia sunsets against gradient blue.
The magenta features a line of busty hula girls.

A year of dating, and they hadn't shown up…
Now they're in the armload I lug from his truck.
A cacophony of wire hangers moves

into my house along with welcomed things:
his sweet-smelling sweaters, walnut armoire,
mouth-blown vase.

I swallow hard at the medicines huddling
on half my vanity, the insulin syringes
taking residence in the fridge.

When I teasingly (but meaning it) insist
the Waikiki Wonders aren't allowed in my closet,
his therapist voice says, *You don't get to choose that.*

My ex let me censor his wardrobe, plan our trips,
cook without butter…then accused me 30 years later
of never letting him have his way.

30 minutes after the shirt remark,
Chris says he likes me caring how he looks.
I had put a note on the door: *Welcome home, baby.*

Now he's seen it, kissed my eyebrow, then my cheek,
then my mouth, I go to throw the paper away,
but he tucks it into his pocket.

At night he's achy. I rub the pressure points along his
spine. For the first time, I can fall asleep pretzeled
with a man, our feet in a pile: alternating his/mine.

Breathing Together

—to Chris, Valentine's Day, 2013

I slide into bed, cold
and you're warm, so warm
you feel like a heating pad
and you say, *Come here*
and fold me in. Soon
my bare body warms, warms
to the same temperature as yours
and you tell me you like the sound
of my breathing as it changes just
before sleep and you even like
my little snore. I was used to
sleeping in my pajamas on opposite
sides of the king-sized bed
(like sleeping in separate neighborhoods)
but you croon that I'm a magnet and you're steel,
and we spoon,
your front to my back
until your arm under my neck falls asleep
and you have to shift.
All night we connect, at least
with a foot or butt to butt
or my hand on your back. In the morning
sometimes, I climb on top of you, not for sex
but to feel the length of my body
on the length of your body,
and you sigh. Your hands glide
along my backbone, and we just stay there—
my back rising as your chest rises, falling
deeper into you as we both exhale.

Prelude

In my head, I practice diligently,
ideas brewing like a Brahms symphony
but creativity often misses its cue.

It breaks out in short Prokofiev notes
(now sonorous, now dissonant),
then fades like the harmonics of a chord.

I sense overtones of something triumphant:
the heralding of Mahler's French horns
or the singing ascension of his strings…

It's as if I'm waiting in the wings,
as if I'm almost ready
to burst forth into my own *Ode to Joy*.

Acknowledgments

I'm grateful for the following publications where previous versions of these poems appeared:

Poetry East: "Drawn into Circles" and "Prelude" (as "Prelude to a Poem")

Your Daily Poem: "Drawn into Circles"

The Best of Poetry Hickory Reading Series (Main Street Rag, 2011): "Drawn into Circles"

Reach of Song (Georgia Poetry Society, 2012): "Drawn into Circles"

Living Above the Frost Line: "Waking Without Alarm"

Skive Magazine (Australia): "Reality Show: Save This Marriage"

Town Creek Poetry: "Visitor"

Falling Star Magazine: "Mating Instincts"

Southern Women's Review: "White after Memorial Day"

"Zumba with Lady Gaga" refers to the following songs, all heard at DWT Dance Studio in Smyrna, GA: Lady Gaga, *Judas;* Kumbia Kings, *Fuego;* Daddy Yankee, *Gasolina;* Unknown musician, unknown song title (*"Jack who's not a ripper"*); Beyoncé, *Single Ladies;* LMFAO, *Sexy and I know It;* Pink, *So What.* "Breathing Together" refers to Walter Egan's song *Magnet and Steel.* "And So It Comes to This" refers to the book, *The High Road Has Less Traffic: Honest Advice on the Path through Love and Divorce* by Monique Honaman.

Big hugs go to my daughter, dogs, siblings and dear friends for living through this story with me and helping me navigate three difficult years. I also give special thanks to my daughter for the front cover graphic.

Thank you to my critique group, the Side Door Poets, for much encouragement and editing help, and to Nancy Simpson and other members of the North Carolina Writers' Network-West who first believed in me as a poet. I also appreciate the poetry teachers who guided and challenged me in workshops over the last four years.

About the Author

Karen Paul Holmes has an MA in music history from the University of Michigan. She eventually moved south and worked her way into a career that involved her love of writing: She became Vice President-Marketing Communications at ING, a global financial services company. Karen is now a freelance writer and owner of two naughty Welsh Terriers.

Karen founded/hosts the Side Door Poets group in Atlanta and Writers' Night Out in the Blue Ridge Mountains. In 2012, she received an Elizabeth George Foundation emerging writer grant for poetry. Her publishing credits include a number of journals and anthologies, including *Poetry East, Atlanta Review, Main Street Rag, Caesura, POEM, The Sow's Ear Poetry Review, American Society: What Poets See* (FutureCycle Press), and the *Southern Poetry Anthology Vol 5: Georgia* (Texas Review Press). You may contact her through her web site: www.simplycommunicated.com.